MARCHING BANDS
Ruth Daly
I0760235
BANDS
LET'S READ
AV2
BY WEIGL
ADDED VALUE • AUDIO VISUAL
www.av2books.com

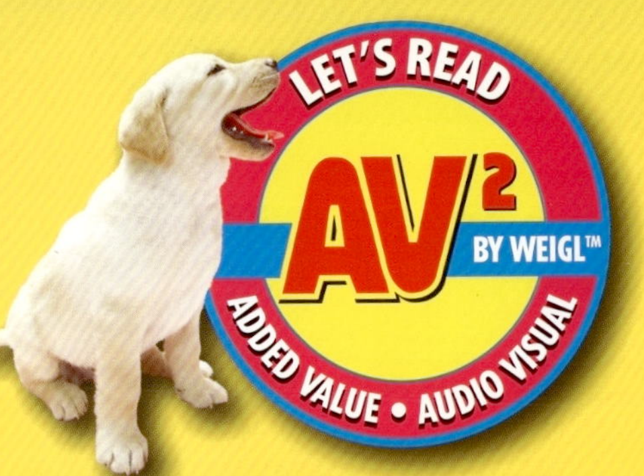

Go to www.av2books.com, and enter this book's unique code.

BOOK CODE

AVQ57454

AV² by Weigl brings you media enhanced books that support active learning.

AV² provides enriched content that supplements and complements this book. Weigl's AV² books strive to create inspired learning and engage young minds in a total learning experience.

Your AV² Media Enhanced books come alive with...

Audio
Listen to sections of the book read aloud.

Video
Watch informative video clips.

Embedded Weblinks
Gain additional information for research.

Try This!
Complete activities and hands-on experiments.

Key Words
Study vocabulary, and complete a matching word activity.

Quizzes
Test your knowledge.

Slide Show
View images and captions, and prepare a presentation.

... and much, much more!

Published by AV² by Weigl
350 5th Avenue, 59th Floor New York, NY 10118
Website: www.av2books.com

Copyright ©2020 AV² by Weigl
All rights reserved. No part of this publication may be reproduced, stored in a retrieval system, or transmitted in any form or by any means, electronic, mechanical, photocopying, recording, or otherwise, without the prior written permission of the publisher.

Library of Congress Control Number: 2019938592

ISBN 978-1-7911-1122-9 (hardcover)
ISBN 978-1-7911-1123-6 (softcover)
ISBN 978-1-7911-1124-3 (multi-user eBook)
ISBN 978-1-7911-1125-0 (single-user eBook)

Printed in Guangzhou, China
1 2 3 4 5 6 7 8 9 0 23 22 21 20 19

062019
311018

Project Coordinator: Heather Kissock Designer: Terry Paulhus

Weigl acknowledges Getty Images, Alamy, Shutterstock, and iStock as the primary image suppliers for this title.

CONTENTS

In this book, you will learn about

- marching bands
- what they are
- where you can see them
- and much more!

Trumpets blare loudly.
Drums pound in time.

Marching bands
are exciting.

CONSTITUTION AV NW
1200
12 ST NW
200
SABRETT
SABRETT

Marching bands tell people that something is happening. People come to see where the music is playing.

SHARIA

Armies had the first marching bands. They helped soldiers march together. They also told soldiers when to fight.

Many bands march to music by John Philip Sousa. He wrote "The Stars and Stripes Forever."

This is the national march of the United States.

John Philip Sousa wrote more than **100 marches.**

YAMAHA
YAMAHA
YAMAHA

A march is a type of song. It is known for its strong beat.

People can walk in time to this beat.

The people in a marching band play different types of instruments. Some play drums. Others play horns.

Flutes and oboes can be part of a marching band, too.

The **tuba** makes the **lowest sounds** in a marching band.

OHIO

The drum major leads the band. He or she carries a long baton. The drum major uses the baton to tell the band what to do.

Marching bands play in parades. They perform at football games. Sometimes, they play for prizes.

The **largest** marching band in the United States has more than **700 members**.

The Rose Parade is held every year.

Marching bands from all over the world take part in it.

ROSE PARADE
presented by
HONDA
Green St
ROSE PARADE
presented by
HONDA

See what you have learned about marching bands.

Which of these pictures is not a marching band?

OHIO

ROSE PARADE
HONDA
ROSE PARADE
HONDA

KEY WORDS

Research has shown that as much as 65 percent of all written material published in English is made up of 300 words. These 300 words cannot be taught using pictures or learned by sounding them out. They must be recognized by sight. This book contains 66 common sight words to help young readers improve their reading fluency and comprehension. This book also teaches young readers several important content words, such as proper nouns. These words are paired with pictures to aid in learning and improve understanding.

Page	Sight Words First Appearance
4	in, time
5	are
7	come, is, people, see, something, tell, that, the, to, where
9	also, first, had, they, together, when
10	and, by, he, many, more, of, than, this
13	a, can, for, it, its, song, walk
14	be, different, makes, others, part, play, some, sounds, too
17	do, long, or, she, uses, what
18	at, has, sometimes
20	all, every, from, over, take, world, year
22	about, have, not, pictures, these, which, you

Page	Content Words First Appearance
4	drums ,trumpets
5	marching bands
7	music
9	armies, soldiers
10	John Philip Sousa, United States
13	beat, song
14	flutes, horns, instruments, oboes, tuba
17	baton, drum major
18	football games, members, parades, prizes
20	Rose Parade

Check out www.av2books.com for activities, videos, audio clips, and more!

1. Go to www.av2books.com.
2. Enter book code. **AVQ57454**
3. Fuel your imagination online!

www.av2books.com